All About PINES

by Irena Freeman
illustrated by Robert Schuster

 HOUGHTON MIFFLIN HARCOURT
School Publishers

Copyright © by Houghton Mifflin Harcourt Publishing Company

Printed in China

ISBN-10: 0-547-25380-X
ISBN-13: 978-0-547-25380-0

5 6 7 8 0940 18 17 16 15 14 13
4500396733

pine trees

snow

When it is winter in the north, it is very cold. White snow covers the ground throughout the forest. Many trees do not have any leaves in the winter. This makes the trees look brown and dead.

But one kind of tree is always green. Pine trees are trees that stay green all winter. It is nice to see something green in the winter.

What makes pine trees different from other trees? Pine trees have pine cones. A pine cone is a hard case for pine tree seeds.

There are many kinds of pine trees. Some are small. The small pine trees are just a little taller than you. Some are very, very tall. The tallest pine trees are called giant redwoods.

Many pine trees grow in places where it is cold in the winter. But some pine trees grow in hot, wet, tropical places.

Redwood

Pine trees can be many different sizes.

Scotch Pine

Man

Eastern White Pine

4

pine cone

pine cone

pine cone

These pine cones come from three different trees.

Pine cones are different. They are not like the seeds or nuts that grow on other trees. That is because there are two kinds of pine cones on every pine tree.

What are the two kinds of pine cones? One kind is a hard cone. The other kind is a soft cone. The hard cones grow on the top of the tree. A tiny pine tree seed can grow inside a hard pine cone.

The soft cones grow lower down on the tree. The soft cones are smaller and softer than hard pine cones. The soft cones make pollen in the spring. Plants need pollen to make new plants. The soft cones die after they make the pollen. Then they fall off the tree.

hard cone

soft cone

The hard pine cones live a long time. They can stay alive for many years. Sometimes some pollen falls on a hard cone. Then it begins to make a seed. The seed can turn into a new pine tree.

The new seed stays inside the pine cone for a long time. Pine tree seeds can stay inside their coverings for years. The pine cone protects the seed.

There are many fires in the forest. The heat from a fire can make a pine cone open up. Then the seed will start to grow after the fire is over.

This shows a forest after a fire. Tiny pine trees will start growing soon.

When pine tree seeds are on the ground, some of the seeds will grow into new pine trees. But it is hard for a tiny new pine tree to grow.

Sometimes the new pine tree does not get enough sunshine. Sometimes it does not absorb enough food from the dirt. A rabbit or deer might eat the new tree.

But if the new pine tree is lucky, it will grow up. Someday the tiny tree will be a big green tree.

deer

new pine trees

rabbit

Deer and rabbits like to eat small pine trees.

candles

This pine tree has many new shoots, called candles.

The weather gets warmer in the spring. Then the pine trees send up new shoots. You can see the shoots at the end of the branches. The shoots are called candles because they look like long candles on a birthday cake.

Pine Needles

Pine needles are the same as leaves.

First the candles grow on the pine tree. Then new pine branches grow at the end of the candles.

Most trees have leaves. Pine trees have leaves too, but they are very, very thin leaves. The leaves on a pine tree are called needles. Pine branches have needles that look like green spines.

The pine needles save, or store light from the sun. Then they turn the sunlight into food for the tree.

What happens to most trees in the fall? The green leaves turn colors. Then they drop off the tree. What happens to pine trees? Most of the green needles stay on the tree. But some pine needles turn brown in the fall. They drop off the pine tree. But the pine needles do not dissolve, or melt into the ground. Pine needles just dry up. You can see clumps of old needles under a pine tree.

Soon the brown needles will fall off this pine tree.

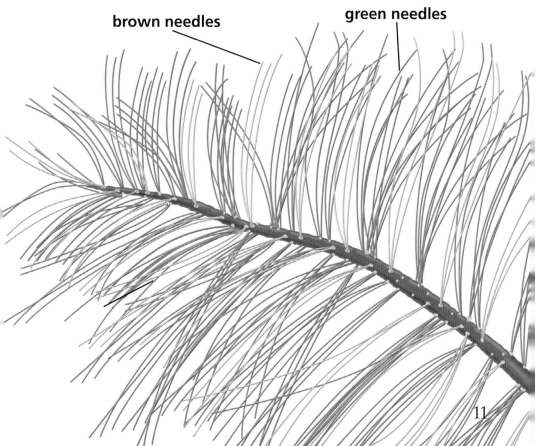

brown needles

green needles

Many things try to kill pine trees. Pine trees can get diseases that make them turn brown and die. Insects can kill all the pine trees in a forest. Animals can chew on the bark and kill the tree.

A fire in the forest can kill pine trees, too. Pine trees can catch on fire in hot, dry weather.

This pine tree is sick.

Many things in a house are made from pine trees.

Pine trees can be made into many different things. The wood from pine trees is used to build houses. The wood is also used to make tables, chairs, and other furniture.

Paper is made out of pine trees. The seeds from pine trees are useful, too. Some people like to eat the seeds!

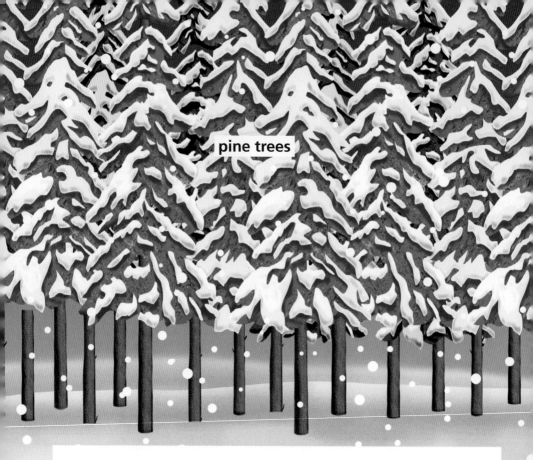

pine trees

People think pine trees are beautiful. People who live in cold places like to plant a row of pine trees. They plant the trees near the house. Then the pine trees stop the cold wind. People can walk through the trees in the snow. The paths are like green passages through the row of trees.

You can go to a forest and listen. You can hear the wind blowing through the pine trees.

Responding

✔ **TARGET SKILL** **Text and Graphic Features** The author of this book used text and graphic features to describe pine trees. Copy the chart below. Complete the chart by writing the purpose of each feature.

Feature captions	Feature labels	Feature needle and leaf shapes
Purpose ?	**Purpose** ?	**Purpose** ?

Write About It

Text to World Think about the many ways people use wood products. Write a paragraph that tells what might happen if there were not enough trees to make things from wood. Include a solution to the problem.

✓ **TARGET SKILL** **Text and Graphic Features**
Tell how words and art work together.

✓ **TARGET STRATEGY** **Question** Ask questions
before you read, while you read, and after you
read.

GENRE Informational text gives factual
information about a topic.